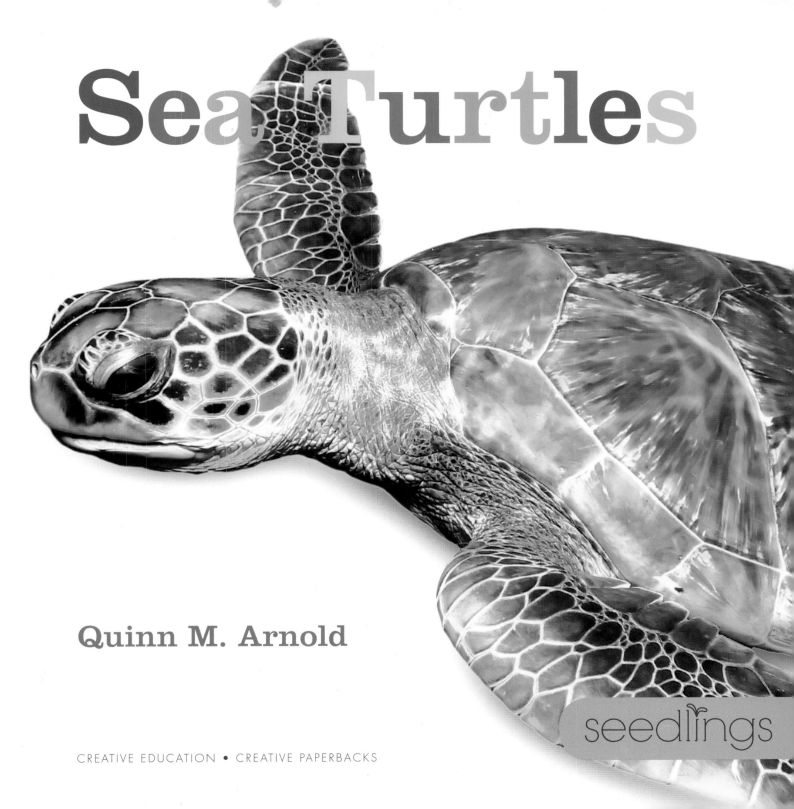

Sea Turtles

Quinn M. Arnold

seedlings

CREATIVE EDUCATION • CREATIVE PAPERBACKS

Published by Creative Education and Creative Paperbacks
P.O. Box 227, Mankato, Minnesota 56002
Creative Education and Creative Paperbacks
are imprints of The Creative Company
www.thecreativecompany.us

Design by Ellen Huber; production by Joe Kahnke
Art direction by Rita Marshall
Printed in the United States of America

Photographs by Alamy (David Fleetham, Amar and Isabelle
Guillen-Guillen Photo LLC), Corbis (Jurgen Freund/Nature Picture
Library, Jason Isley-Scubazoo/Science Faction, Monica & Michael
Sweet/Design Pics, Michele Westmorland), Dreamstime (2tamsalu,
Richard Carey, Divehive, Isabellebonaire, Eugene Kalenkovich),
Getty Images (Pete Atkinson, Reinhard Dirscherl, M. M. Sweet),
iStockphoto (WhitcombeRD), National Geographic Creative (JOEL
SARTORE), Shutterstock (abcphotosystem, Rich Carey, James A
Dawson, Isabelle Kuehn)

Library of Congress Cataloging-in-Publication Data
Arnold, Quinn M.
Sea Turtles / Quinn M. Arnold.
p. cm. — (Seedlings)
Includes bibliographical references and index.
Summary: A kindergarten-level introduction to sea turtles,
covering their growth process, behaviors, the oceans they call
home, and such defining features as their long front flippers.
ISBN 978-1-60818-780-5 (hardcover)
ISBN 978-1-62832-400-6 (pbk)
ISBN 978-1-56660-834-3 (eBook)
This title has been submitted for
CIP processing under LCCN 2016937125.

CCSS: RI.K.1, 2, 3, 4, 5, 6, 7;
RI.1.1, 2, 3, 4, 5, 6, 7; RF.K.1, 3; RF.1.1

First Edition HC 9 8 7 6 5 4 3 2 1
First Edition PBK 9 8 7 6 5 4 3 2 1

TABLE OF CONTENTS

Hello,
sea turtles!

Seven kinds of sea turtles live in Earth's oceans.

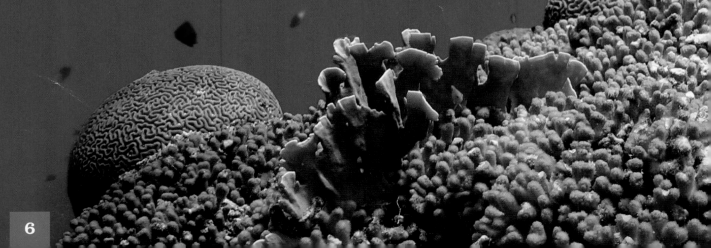

They swim and sleep in the salty water.

Long front flippers help a turtle swim.

Its shell keeps it safe.

Some sea turtles
hide under rocks.

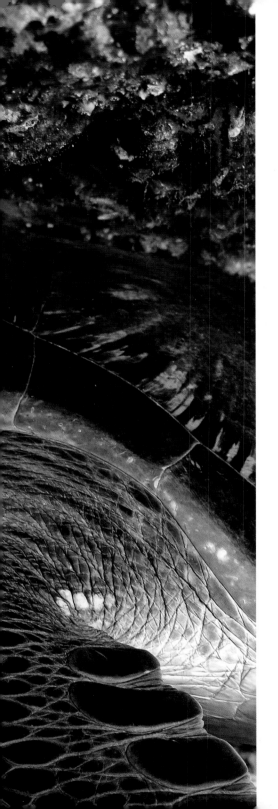

They can hold their breath a long time!

Sea turtles smell food with their nose. Green sea turtles eat only plants.

Other turtles eat crabs and jellyfish.

Sea turtles lay their eggs on a beach. Hatchlings dig out of the nest.

They crawl to the water.

Sea turtles live alone.

Leatherbacks
swim thousands
of miles. They dive
deep in the ocean.

Goodbye,
sea turtles!

Picture a Sea Turtle

shell

tail

flipper

20

nostril

beak

eye

21

flippers: flat limbs (like arms) that help sea turtles swim

hatchlings: baby sea turtles

oceans: big areas of deep, salty water

Read More

Marsh, Laura. *Sea Turtles*.
Washington, D.C.: National Geographic, 2011.

Perkins, Wendy. *Sea Turtle*.
Mankato, Minn.: Amicus, 2012.

Websites

National Wildlife Federation: Fruit Sea Turtle
http://www.nwf.org/kids/family-fun/recipes/fruit-turtle.aspx
Use fruit to make your own sea turtle.

Sea Turtle Conservancy: Kids Corner
http://www.conserveturtles.org/turtletides.php
Take sea turtle quizzes and print pictures to color.

Index